THE DAVID DEBT MANAGEMENT PLAN

Charleston, SC
www.PalmettoPublishing.com

The David Debt Management Plan
Copyright © 2023 by Bishop Walter Richard Ellerbe, D.D.

All rights reserved

No portion of this book may be reproduced, stored in a retrieval system, or transmitted in any form by any means—electronic, mechanical, photocopy, recording, or other—except for brief quotations in printed reviews, without prior permission of the author.

Paperback ISBN: 979-8-8229-1712-5
eBook ISBN: 979-8-8229-1713-2

THE DAVID DEBT MANAGEMENT PLAN

Bishop Walter Richard Ellerbe, D.D.

This book is dedicated to my late parents, Deacon Wade T. and Mary E. Ellerbe Smith; to my late father- and mother-in-law, Rev. June and Mildred Hamilton; and to my adopted parents, Deacon Robert and Addie Pickett. These people were the ones influential to my life.

TABLE OF CONTENTS

Introduction 1

Chapter 1
    Defining Debt 3
    Debt Canceled 4
    David Anointed 5
    David Sent to Check on His Brothers (1 Samuel 17:16–31) 6

Chapter 2
    Goliath the Giant (1 Samuel 17:1–11) 8
        His Prodigious Size 8
        His Armor 8
        His Challenge 9
        The Terror He Struck 9
    David's Reaction (1 Samuel 17:24–6) 9

Chapter 3
    What Causes Debt? 11
    Financial Bondage 11
    Circumventing God's Will 12
        Using Human Instead of Divine Methods 12
        Becoming the Slave of a Lending Institution 12
        Becoming a Slave to Big Givers 13
        Becoming Trapped by Financial Pressure 13
        Becoming Mired in an Endless Cycle of Borrowing 13
        Losing Flexibility to Respond to Ministry Opportunities 14

Chapter 4
    David's Challenge (1 Samuel 17:31–54)   15
        Don't Be Afraid   15
        Thy Servant Will Go   16
        Thy Servant Will Fight   17
    Saul's Response (1 Samuel 17:33)   17
    David's Testimony (1 Samuel 17:3–37)   18

Chapter 5
    The Description of the Lion and Bear   19
    The Lion   19
    The Bear   20
    God's Deliverance   21
    David Used His Hands   22

Chapter 6
    Comparing the Lion and Bear with Debt   23
        Small Bills   23
    Saul Was Convinced (Doing Things the World's Way)   24

Chapter 7
    David's Complaint (1 Samuel 17:39)   26
    David Prepared (Doing Things the Lord's Way,
        1 Samuel 17:40)   28
        His Staff   28
        Five Smooth Stones   28
        His Sling   29

Chapter 8
    Goliath's Reaction (1 Samuel 17:41–44)   31
    David's Response (1 Samuel 17:45–47)   32
        Operate in the Name of the Lord   32
        Acknowledge Who the Lord Is   33
        Realize that Debt Brings Shame   33

Chapter 9
    David Prophesied (1 Samuel 17:46–47)   34
        The Lord Will Deliver You into My Hand   35
        I Will Kill You and Cut Your Head Off   35
        I Will Give Your Body to the Birds and Wild Beasts   35

Chapter 10
    Why Pay off Debt? (1 Samuel 17:46b–47)   36
    David Faced the Giant (1 Samuel 17:48)   37
    David Was Prepared (1 Samuel 17:49)   37
        He Had What He Needed   38
        He Was Able to Produce the Object That Killed the Giant   38
        He Used the Object Properly   39
        He Had More Than Enough   39

Chapter 11
    Prophecy fulfilled (1 Samuel 17:50–51)   40
        David Prevailed Over Goliath the Giant   40
        Defeating the Giant Brought Joy   41
    Conclusion of the Matter (1 Samuel 17:54–55, 57)   41

Acknowledgments   43

INTRODUCTION

This book will focus on how to deal with debt by following the example of the life of David, whom God anointed and appointed through the prophet Samuel . David set the example for the believer to cancel debt using a simple but powerful procedure. His success of killing a lion, a bear, and eventually Goliath the giant offers evidence that, if followed in the arena of managing one's money, will cancel debt from the smallest account to the largest account, thus giving the person access to financial freedom. Once freedom is achieved, it will free up monies for ministry for the advancement of the kingdom of God as well as for personal desires and goals.

Because David was responsible for keeping his father's sheep, he found himself engaging in battle with a lion and a bear. God proved to David that He had provided him the necessary strength to protect the sheep in his care. As a result, David discovered that God was able to deliver him in any given situation. David's father sent him to check on his brothers and King Saul, who were in battle with the Philistines. To David's amazement, he found Saul and the Israelite army hiding from the Philistine army because of the giant Goliath.

Goliath enjoyed challenging Israel each day for forty days. He used his huge stature and ability to frighten the Israelite army into thinking there was no hope for them. God used David, who was then a young boy described as being "ruddy and of a fair countenance" (1 Samuel 17:42), to deliver Israel out of the hands of the giant. We can use David's example to deal with debt that has the church, the Body of Christ, in hiding and afraid to face our creditors. We will find that God has the ability through our availability to conquer the inevitable.

CHAPTER 1

Defining Debt

Debt is something owed to another. It is a liability or obligation to pay or render something. Debt causes one to be under obligation to another until all notes are paid. Debt is deferred payment, accounts receivable, deficit, default, nonpayment, and money borrowed . In a stricter, more traditional, more biblical sense, debt would be defined as a neglect or violation of duty. Indebtedness occurs when one's accounts are in arrears, or when one is behind in payments. In a biblical sense, debt refers to those who have broken their promise or vow and either will not or cannot repay what they owe. The church was not built to follow the pattern of the world. God has established in His Word that we are to be prime examples for the world, and that includes paying off debt in a timely manner.

The nation of Israel was in debt as they hid from an uncircumcised giant who frightened them. It was not that they owed the Philistines anything other than defending themselves; rather they owed God because they had not come out to fight. If they were truly walking in the favor of God, then they should have destroyed the giant and all the Philistines immediately upon arriving in that valley. But because Saul had not the "favor of God," the army did not have God's presence and power to resist the giant. *Fear* set in because *faith* had moved out. God had ordained that, at the end of forty days, David would show up to show Israel that God is a debt-canceling God.

Debt Canceled

God allowed Israel to borrow from the Egyptians jewels of silver, jewels of gold, and raiment because they had what rightfully belonged to the Israelites. For more than 430 years, Israel had slaved under the new Pharaoh and did not receive honest wages for their devotion to the building of Egypt. When Moses was sent to Pharaoh to deliver a message of freedom, Pharaoh made it more difficult for Israel to escape (Exodus 5:9). When the time of departure was upon them, God caused the Israelites to find favor in the sight of the Egyptians so that they were told that they would not go out empty-handed. God had promised that "every woman shall borrow from her neighbors, and jewels of silver, and jewels of gold, and raiment would be given to them." They were told to place them "on their sons and daughters and prepare to spoil the Egyptians" (Ex. 3:21–22). After Israel received these items, God delivered them from Egypt. God canceled their debt at the Red Sea by drowning the Egyptian army. Moses declared that they would not see the Egyptians again after that particular day (Ex. 14:13).

Israel witnessed God's destroying of the Egyptian army that trailed them on the path through the waters. Once the Egyptians were in the midst of the Red Sea, God had Moses repeat the same procedure that had caused the sea to open. Moses stretched out his rod and the sea closed upon the Egyptians. They were drowned, every one of them, thus the prophecy was fulfilled that the Israelites would not see the Egyptians again. More importantly, the debt was cancelled concerning the borrowing of the valuables they had received before leaving Egypt. One cannot pay back a person who no longer exists.

David Anointed

God grew tired of King Saul's disobedience and instructed Samuel to go to Jesse's house to anoint one of his sons as king of Israel (1 Sam. 16). Samuel obeyed God and made haste to Jesse's house. He requested that Jesse bring out his sons before him so he could anoint the one God approved. Samuel viewed each son and felt that surely God would want to anoint any one of these fine, strong, and robust young men. God informed Samuel not to look on the outer appearance, for God was looking at the heart (1 Sam. 16:7). Eventually, Samuel had viewed seven of Jesse's sons, and God had not given him the okay to anoint any of them. Samuel asked Jesse, "Do you have any more sons available for me to look at?" Jesse responded, "I have one more who's down in the pasture tending to the sheep" (1 Sam. 16:11). Samuel had the young man summoned to come quickly to see if he would be the one to anoint.

When young David arrived on the scene, God told Samuel that he was the one to anoint. Samuel poured the oil upon David, David became the anointed of the Lord, and the Spirit of the Lord came upon David from that day forward (1 Sam. 16:13). David, of course, did not even compare to the stature of his brothers. He was ruddy with a beautiful countenance, good to look at. David was only a youth, but God ordered Samuel to anoint him as the next king of Israel. God took the last, the youngest, the smallest, and the least qualified to do His bidding. God's way of working is the opposite of man's. Israel wanted a king like all the other nations, and God gave them what they wanted. He gave them Saul, a man much taller than any other man who would stand above everyone else. He gave them someone who would think big and act importantly in his decision-making. King Saul's decisions, however, caused the Israelites to be in debt and hiding rather than walking in victory.

For many reasons, God chose David as king, but God wanted to show Israel that He could do the impossible with the least powerful. God used Gideon, who was the least in his tribe, to bring deliverance to the Israelites when they were in bondage to the Midianites. God diminished an army of 32,000 with a mere 300 soldiers to show them that he could save with the least (Judg. 7:1–7).

In a similar way, the small amount that is overlooked in finances can help deliver one from financial despair. If Samuel had overlooked David, then God's order would have not been followed. For this reason, I have been led to share with you the experiences that David encountered with the lion, the bear, and Goliath the giant to give order to debt cancellation. I believe that if one follows what David experienced, they can come out of debt with the head of the giant in their hand.

David Sent to Check on His Brothers (1 Samuel 17:16–31)

David's father Jesse told him to check on his brothers. He was to take corn and bread to his brothers and to give Saul some cheese. First Samuel 16 states that the giant Goliath presented himself for forty days to challenge the army of Israel. This suggests that at the end of forty days, it is time for this taunting to come to a halt. After forty days, God had delivered to Moses the Ten Commandments that would give guidance to His people (Ex. 34:28). At the end of forty days of fasting in the wilderness, God allowed His Son to be tempted by the devil (Matt. 4:1–3). It is the end of forty days that Goliath has challenged Israel; it is time to deal with this giant in comparison to debt, and resolve it conclusively.

CHAPTER 1

As his father had instructed him, David rose early the next morning, left the sheep with a keeper, and went to the battle to deliver the food to his brothers and King Saul. As he approached the scene of the battle, he came to the trench as the army was going forth. At this particular time, everything was somewhat on hold. For forty days the Israelites remained in the trenches and watched Goliath the giant come out and challenge them. As the challenge went on, the Israelite army was terrified. They felt that there was not a man to go out and defeat the giant, not even Saul.

CHAPTER 2

Goliath the Giant (1 Samuel 17:1–11)

His Prodigious Size

The learned Bishop Cumberland says that the scripture cubit was about twenty-one inches, and a span was half a cubit. By this computation, Goliath was approximately eleven feet, four inches tall: a monstrous stature. This is almost twice the height of an ordinary man.

His Armor

Goliath wore a helmet of brass on his head, a coat of mail made of brass plates laid over one another like the scales of a fish, and, because his legs were within the reach of an ordinary man, brass boots. He also had a large corselet of brass around his neck. The coat of mail is said to weigh 5,000 shekels (more than 150 pounds). But some think this number refers not to the weight of the coat but to the value of it. Goliath's offensive weapons were extraordinary; only his spear is described here, as a weaver's beam. His arm could manage what an ordinary man could scarcely heave. His esquire carried his shield before him.

CHAPTER 2

His Challenge
The Philistines chose Goliath for their champion. To save themselves from the hazard of a battle, they stood and cried unto the armies of Israel, challenging them to send a man out to fight with their giant.

The Terror He Struck
The sight of Goliath struck terror upon Israel. Saul and all his army were greatly afraid. The people would not have been dismayed if they had not observed Saul's courage failing him. If the leader is a coward, the followers should be bold, but they were terrified.

David's Reaction (1 Samuel 17:24–6)

When David saw this, he inquired as to what would be done for the man who would kill the giant in order to take away the reproach (shame) from Israel (1 Sam. 17:26). Furthermore, David acknowledged that Goliath was an uncircumcised Philistine who was defying (standing against) the armies of the living God! In response to David's questions, he found that a reward would be given to the man who could defeat the giant: the king would give him great riches, and would give him his daughter, and make his father's house free in Israel (1 Sam. 17:25). It was not this reward that gave David the determination to take Goliath's challenge but the fact that the name of the living God was being brought to shame. David knew that God was the God of Israel.

In canceling debt, it should be more than a reward to us to be out of debt. It should be that God's name is held in high regard because we don't owe anyone anything other than to love them (Rom. 13:8). Really, it is all about God's name. When something concerns His name, it then concerns our name, for "a good name is rather to be chosen than great riches, and loving favor than silver and gold" (Prov. 22:1).

Debt canceling is about keeping the name of God free and clear. We know that God cannot be charged foolishly, but because we are believers, what we do foolishly can be attributed to God wrongfully because of our neglect to trust God. As a result, David was determined not to allow the name of God to suffer shame or to allow Israel to be seen as a nation of defeat.

CHAPTER 3

What Causes Debt?

Debt occurs when you do not manage the money you make and allow yourself to purchase items that cannot be covered because there is not enough money coming in to support such purchases. Debt that cannot be paid will ultimately cause problems. You will be prone to borrow from lending institutions that advertise their services. Because you do not have the financial resources to cover your indebtedness, you are most likely to take them up on their offer. Being in debt will pressure you to borrow, and borrowing will cause you to become the "servant to the lender," and "the tail and not the head" (Prov. 22:7; Deut. 28:13).

Financial Bondage

Another way to describe this problem is the loss of freedom. In Proverbs 22:7, the Bible depicts indebtedness as enslavement. This verse is one of the Bible's strongest cautions regarding the risks of borrowing: "The rich rule over the poor, and the borrower is servant to the lender." It is presented in Scripture toward the end of a long collection of Solomon's wisdom on a wide variety of practical subjects. Much of his advice is presented in the form of cause and effect. Proverbs 22:7 is a perfect example. If you sow borrowing, you will harvest slavery. In the case of Israel hiding from the Philistines, they sowed neglect in following God's instruction, and they now are reaping the need to hide from the enemy.

Circumventing God's Will

The Bible teaches that God is sovereign. He has everything in the universe under His benevolent control. However, people also have choices, and they can do things that are contrary to God's principles and desires. In the materialistic American culture, the abuse of easy credit is one of the most deceptive ways to run away from and fight against God's direction in the lives of Christians.

Using Human Instead of Divine Methods
Borrowing from lenders is a worldly approach to ministry and not a divine one. One of the dangers of borrowing is that it enables ministries to appear "successful" beyond the actual means God has entrusted to them. When you fund ministry through borrowing, your ministry "success" is measured not by how generously people give but by how much the bank is willing to lend.

Becoming the Slave of a Lending Institution
Again, according to Proverbs 22:7, those who borrow become the slaves of their lenders. When you borrow, the issue is not whether you are in slavery but what kind of taskmaster you must serve. Some lenders are relatively kind taskmasters who demand little. Others are harsh and exacting, requiring much, regardless of how little you have. Church management consultant David Pollock warns, "When your church

borrows, you automatically reorder all of its priorities. Debt becomes an 800-pound gorilla that sits on the platform of the church and demands to be fed every week. Because of the laws in this country, you have to pay the debt as your first and foremost priority." Or debt becomes a giant like Goliath who comes out and challenges you every single day. Because it has grown so tremendously, it has you terrified and in hiding.

Becoming a Slave to Big Givers
When a ministry borrows, its supporters become pressured to give because the financial obligation must be met. And when the pressure is on, ministry leaders too often look to the ministry's big givers for extra help. The apostle Paul, paraphrasing Job 41:11, says in Romans 11:35, "Who has ever given to God, that God should repay him?" God is obliged to no one, and control over Christ's body cannot be bought.

Becoming Trapped by Financial Pressure
Financial pressure and worry are constant afflictions in many loan-funded ministries. It is reported that people have tension, anxiety, factions, and unrest within congregations because of debt . Having to repay loans will invade your personal devotional times , making it difficult to effectively read the Bible or pray. In other words, if you are obligated to pay your creditor, and the funds are limited; this will more likely limit your time with God!

Becoming Mired in an Endless Cycle of Borrowing
Contrary to what many believe, you can't borrow your way out of debt. Borrowing too often becomes financial quicksand—once you get caught, it is difficult to break free. The perceived "need" to borrow sometimes becomes a runaway train with momentum of its own.

Losing Flexibility to Respond to Ministry Opportunities
When a ministry is repaying loans with interest, it is difficult to respond to unforeseen ministry needs. This is one of the most frequently cited reasons that ministries pay off their loans and adopt a non-borrowing policy.

CHAPTER 4

David's Challenge (1 Samuel 17:31–54)

Don't Be Afraid

When the words of David were told to Saul—that David would take the challenge of the giant—Saul sent for David and asked him to share his thoughts. David was convinced that he would defeat the giant. His exact words were, "Let no man's heart fail because of him; thy servant will go and fight with this Philistine" (1 Sam. 17:32). The first point to consider is that David viewed himself as God's servant. If we are going to defeat the giants in life, we must know that we are God's servants sent to do His will. As a servant, you never lose sight of servanthood. Know that God is the Master, and He alone will provide for the servant to do His bidding. If the Master has given you permission to accomplish a certain task, it will certainly be carried out to the fullest, most successful extent. You need not be afraid.

David knew his role in life. Back at home, he did exactly what his father Jesse ordered him to do. He never came to the forefront to be viewed by Samuel until his father sent for him. Meanwhile, he remained with the sheep to guard, feed, and carefully watch them, making sure no predators would come and harm his father's herd. David ran errands for his father and did not complain. He availed himself to every task his father wanted done. When Jesse sent David to check on his brothers and see how they were getting along, David did not hesitate. When David stood before King Saul, he had courage and felt that he was part of the confrontation.

"Thy servant will go," David said to the king, in reference to fighting the giant. David was basically employing himself in the Israelite army. "Since I am here, I might as well make myself useful (1 Sam. 17:32)." David saw that no one else was making any effort to confront the giant, so he might as well do so.

David was not concerned at the moment of his age, about not having a uniform, or about not having weapons such as soldiers should have. Nor did he concern himself about how big the giant was. He was highly upset that this Philistine had the people of God in hiding.

Thy Servant Will Go
David made it known that he was a servant to Saul. In 1 Samuel 16:14–23, we find that David was summoned to provide music for Saul, especially when he was irritated and in bad spirits. The music would calm and refresh Saul, and the evil spirit would leave him. David became Saul's armor-bearer. He was already employed on Saul's staff; he just was not old enough to enlist in the army. When it came time to go off to war, David's three oldest brothers—Eliab, Abinadab, and Shammah—were commissioned to go fight against the Philistines, while David returned home to feed his father's sheep in Bethlehem (1 Sam. 17:13–15).

God will always make room for His servant to be used by Him so that His name will be manifested abroad. God was focused not on the three eldest sons of Jesse but on the servanthood of David. The anointing on his life would glorify God in this situation.

CHAPTER 4

Thy Servant Will Fight

David was willing to risk his life against the giant. He had faith in God that he could accomplish this awesome task. He was not focused on the size of the giant; he was focused on the power of God, who was much bigger than the giant. David said, "I will go and fight with this Philistine" (1 Sam. 17:32). In a similar way, we must be willing to face the debt that has forced us to hide and not come out. It is not God's will for the people of God to have a spirit of fear: "For God hath not given us the spirit of fear; but of power, and of love, and of a sound mind" (2 Tim. 1:7).

David operated in the power of God, in the love of God, and with a sound mind. He was fully aware of what he was saying. He was conscious of the fact that this giant was well over eleven feet tall and covered surrounded by armor, with a shield in front of him. David did not focus on the physical being of this giant; rather he focused on the ability of God, who had not failed him in various situations.

Saul's Response (1 Samuel 17:33)

Saul said to David, "Thou art not able to go against this Philistine to fight with him: for thou art but a youth, and he a man of war from his youth (1 Samuel 17:33)." In other words, "You are too young. This man has been fighting ever since he was a youth and has experience in what he is doing. You are just a youth and are not even old enough to enlist in the army. You have no experience in fighting, and certainly you don't have the slightest clue as to defeating a man of his caliber." Saul was doing as he always had done, assessing the situation by common sense. He compared David's life with the life of the giant. This prompted David to share his testimony of his previous deliverances.

David's Testimony (1 Samuel 17:3–37)

David shared with Saul what had taken place in the pasture before this present situation: "Thy servant kept his father's sheep, and there came a lion, and a bear, and took a lamb out of the flock: And I went out after him, and smote him, and delivered it out of his mouth: and when he arose against me, I caught him by his beard, and smote him, and slew him. Thy servant slew both the lion and the bear: and this uncircumcised Philistine shall be as one of them, seeing he hath defied the armies of the living God...The Lord that delivered me out of the paw of the lion, and out of the paw of the bear, he will deliver me out of the hand of this Philistine."

David was young, but something took place on the day when Samuel anointed him. Ever since that day, David was never the same. David defeated a lion and a bear, and he was anxious to add the giant to his list.

People can deal with debt in the way David dealt with the lion, the bear, and eventually the giant. We will compare each opponent with levels of debt to prove that those who follow the way David handled his situation can liquidate debt over a period of time.

CHAPTER 5

The Description of the Lion and Bear

The Lion

The lion is a big, powerful feline. It is probably the most famous member of the feline family. People are frightened by the lion's thundering roar and impressed by its strength and royal appearance. The lion is called the king of beasts and is a well-known symbol of beauty and power. Most lions live in woodlands, grassy plains, and areas with thorny scrub trees.

Along with the tiger, the lion is among the largest members of the feline family. Lions are built for strength, not speed. A male lion usually weighs 350 to 400 pounds, but some weigh up to 500 pounds. Most males are about nine feet long from the nose to the end of the tail. They are about three and a half feet tall at the shoulder. The female lions are smaller than males. They weigh only 250 to 300 pounds and are about a foot shorter.

The Bear

CHAPTER 5

All bears belong to the family Ursidae. They are found largely in northern temperate regions and are widely distributed in North America, Europe, and Asia. Many species of bears display physical characteristics adapted to their particular environments. Some of the major species of are the American black bear, the brown bear, the grizzly bear, and the polar bear. These are considered to be the largest of the bears in their species. The brown bear is the most common of bears and the largest flesh-eating land mammal. Scientists agree that the North American brown bear, the Eur asian brown bear, and the grizzly are closely related. The grizzly bear is also known as the silvertip bear and is the fiercest animal in North America. It is strong enough to carry small horses and cattle. The brown bear and the grizzly, both range from 88 feet to 99 feet in length and from 350 pounds to 1,720 pounds.

David might have had confrontations with either the grizzly bear or the brown bear. They were located in Europe and the Middle East according to *The World Book Encyclopedia*. According to David's testimony, it must have been the grizzly bear that carried away one of his sheep.

God's Deliverance

In David's testimony, he declared that a lion and a bear tried to make off with one of his father's sheep. This perhaps took place on more than one occasion. However, once David saw that the sheep's life was in danger, he came to its rescue. David reported that when he confronted the lion, the beast rose up against him and tried to prevent him from recovering the sheep. David then took the lion by the "beard" with his bare hands and broke its neck. On another occasion, a bear tried the same trick. David once again discovered that a bear was trying to escape with one of his father's sheep. He confronted the bear, and the bear rose up on its hind legs to strike David. With his bare hands, David took the bear by the hair and broke its neck.

David realized that God had provided the necessary strength to destroy both the lion and the bear. He had gained confidence from his experiences of the Lord's previous deliverances on his behalf. Further, since God would not allow His reputation to be damaged by this Philistine giant, David was certain that God would again deliver him in this trial by conflict. God delivered David from the lion and the bear that tried to destroy David's father's sheep, and now God would deliver him from the giant trying to destroy God's sheep, the Israelite army.

David Used His Hands

When David said he smote the bear, it is assumed that he either used his bare hands or he used his sling. Either way, it suggests that people must be willing to use their hands or whatever they have on hand to get out of debt . Through Moses, the Lord informed the children of Israel that He would bless them in all their works and in all that they put their *hand* unto (Deut. 15:10b). Paul pleaded with the Ephesians who stole to "steal no more: rather let him labor, working with his *hands* the thing which is good, that he may have to give to him that needeth" (Eph. 4:28, italics added). Paul also made reference "that ye study to be quiet, and to do your own business, and to work with your own hands, as we commanded you; (I Thessalonians 4:11). Of course, we know that the anointing upon David is what made the difference; it provided a supernatural breakthrough when otherwise, in the natural world, he would have been defeated .

CHAPTER 6

Comparing the Lion and Bear with Debt

The lion that David slew represents the smallest bills in your expenditures that you are trying to pay off. The bear represents the next largest bills that you are indebted to pay. You cannot pay off the large debts until you have paid off the smaller debts. Once you have accomplished this, it will build your faith to handle bigger debts that need to be paid off. David sets the example for the believer in his struggles with the lion and the bear. From him, we learn that the believer must have God's anointing upon his or her life to go up against the odds. After the anointing is upon one's life, they are now ready to address the attacker and defeat it in the name of Jesus.

Small Bills

Many Christians, who are in debt, don't have large debts that weigh them down. Instead, they have several small debts that are like small cuts or toothaches that go unnoticed because they focus on the larger bills. If you take the David Debt Management approach, you will find it much easier to deal with your debts.

Administering medicine and bandages to small cuts and abstracting teeth that bring discomfort will provide relief and deliverance so a person can focus on larger, more demanding problems. Small wounds are just as important as bigger ones, and if they go unnoticed, infection and gangrene can set in, putting a person in harm's way and even causing death. Debt can act in a comparable way.

When David watched his father's sheep, he was responsible for every sheep in the pasture and did not want to lose one. In an earlier time, when Jacob kept his father-in-law's sheep, he replaced every one that died or was killed or stolen (Gen. 31:38–39). These men watched over animals. Jesus, on the other hand, dealt with the sheep of his Father, the disciples. He prayed to his Father to report the account of the men whom he had taught and trained (Jn. 17:12). When we realize that everything God gives to us is important and that we are stewards of all and owners of nothing, then we will appreciate and take care of God's property. This includes working our way out of debt.

Saul Was Convinced (Doing Things the World's Way)

Convinced by David's testimony concerning the extermination of the lion and the bear, King Saul allowed him to go out against the Philistine giant. But Saul gave David "his" armor. The word "his" denotes the world's way of dealing with or preparing for struggles. Saul gave him these items:

1. His armor
2. His helmet of brass
3. His coat of mail
4. His sword

CHAPTER 6

As David prepared to go out to meet the giant Goliath, he realized that the king's armor did not fit him. It did not fit, nor did it feel right. The world has a way of handling debt. Most of the time, debtors are offered plans that will only put them in more debt and bondage. These programs pay off consolidated debt and offer low monthly payments, but the interest is normally fixed at a high rate, and in the end, you will pay back more than you owed at the outset. If what you are trying on doesn't fit, do not keep trying it. If what you are about to embark upon to bail yourself out of debt does not feel right, leave it alone.

I remember when my wife and I were trying to restore our home. Our home is debt free. We wanted to use the deed to our home as collateral for a loan to remodel the house. Little did we know that the approved loan was at a 15 percent fixed interest rate over a twenty-year period. The loan was approximately $10,000. Our payments were about $150 per month. Paying this amount over a twenty-year period would have eventually cost us $36,000, almost three times more than we were borrowing. Thanks be unto God for the Holy Spirit because I did not feel right about the proposal, called the lenders, and canceled the plan at the last moment. If you don't feel right about something, most of the time it is not right. And if it does not feel right, don't do it!

CHAPTER 7

David's Complaint (1 Samuel 17:39)

David did not want to disrespect King Saul, but the suit of armor did not feel right. He was uncomfortable and could not balance himself in such an outfit. David complained, "I cannot go with these; for I have not proved them (1 Samuel 17:39)."

And he took off the armor. David was not used to solving problems the way Saul and the soldiers were accustomed to doing. More importantly, the anointing in his life went against the world's way. David was not ashamed to remove the armor; he "put them off him (I Samuel 17:39b)." He was dealing with reality. In reality, he knew that Saul's way was not the way God had delivered him in the past, out of the paw of the lion and out of the paw of the bear. God had supernaturally delivered David in the previous situations, and David depended on God to do the same now.

Whatever one has depended on to deliver them in the past is what they will expect to deliver them in any other situation. When it comes to finances, most of society adheres to a line of credit and gets deeper into debt. They have their needs met at the moment, but to their disappointment, when the bill arrives, they will be dismayed. David knew

CHAPTER 7

that what the king offered was not involved in God's previous deliverances. Therefore, David had to be light and comfortable to fight with the giant. If David had tried to go out and fight with that armor on, the giant would have crushed him. Saul's armor would have hindered David, altering his style of operation and ultimately bringing about his demise.

When you are trying to solve your financial problems, you must put off the world's way like David put off Saul's armor. Here are some tips:

- Get rid of multiple credit cards
- Buy on credit only occasionally
- Avoid going right back into debt once old debts are paid
- Stop buying on first response and pray about it first
- Take care of what is owned and save your money to buy something new with cash
- Make a budget and stick with it
- Stop responding to preapproved credit card companies
- Stop dealing with companies that advertise "No Credit, Slow Credit, Bad Credit"

When David put on Saul's pieces of armor, he said he had "not proved them." Proved means to give demonstration or proof of something by action; to establish the genuineness or validity of something; to subject something to some testing process. It means to confirm or to verify. In most cases, you will respond to what you are familiar with or what you have tried repeatedly. When David killed the lion and the bear, he knew that God was in charge.

David Prepared
(Doing Things the Lord's Way, 1 Samuel 17:40)

David took the items that he was most familiar with : his staff, five smooth stones out of the brook, and his sling to go and defeat the Giant!

His Staff

A staff is also called a rod, which designates a straight, slender stick growing on or cut from a tree (Gen. 30:37–41; Jer. 1:11). The word "rod" is sometimes used interchangeably with "staff" (Is. 10:5; Rev. 11:1). Rods and staffs were used in several ways:

1. As walking sticks (Gen. 32:10) and for defense (Ps. 23:4)

2. For punishment (Ex. 21:20; Numbers 22:27; Pr. 13:24; 1 Cor. 4:21)

3. For measurement (Rev. 11:1)

4. As symbols of prophetic office (Ex. 4:2–4; 7:8–24; Judg. 6:21)

5. As symbols of priestly office (Num. 17:1–10)

6. As symbols of royal office (Gen. 49:10; Judg. 5:14; Jer. 48:17; Rev. 2:27)

In David's case, his staff would represent all the above. The anointing of God upon David's life gave him the privilege to act in all of these ways.

Five Smooth Stones

A stone is part of the hardened mineral matter that comprises much of the earth. In biblical times, large single stones were used to close the mouths of cisterns, wells, and tombs (Gen. 29:2; Matt. 27:60; Jn. 11:38). They were also used to mark boundaries (Deut. 19:14). The

CHAPTER 7

Israelites sometimes consecrated a single stone as a memorial to God (Gen. 28:18–22; 1 Sam. 7:12). Stones were also used as lethal weapons (1 Sam. 17:49; Acts 7:58). David chose five smooth stones to represent the *Pentateuch*, the first five books of the Old Testament.

The word *Pentateuch* comes from two Greek words, *penta* meaning "five" and *teuchos* meaning "box," "jar," or "scroll." Originally the word was used as an adjective meaning "a five-scrolled (book)." The common Jewish arrangement calls the first five books of the Hebrew Bible "Torah," which means law or teaching. The one stone David used would represent the book of Exodus. Why Exodus? This book addresses coming out of debt. The Israelites were in bondage for 430 years. That type of bondage is similar to their situation in 1 Samuel, where they are hiding from the Philistine army because of the giant. Exodus means "going out" or "coming out." David was convinced that God had brought the Israelites out and wanted them to stay out. Exodus also includes the story of the rock that Israel drank from (Ex. 17:5–6). And the New Testament declares that the Rock was Jesus (1 Cor. 10:4).

His Sling

A sling is a weapon of two long straps with a piece between them at the ends to hold a stone. The slinger twirled the pocketed missile above his head. Once he released one of the straps, the stone was ejected toward its victim. The blow disarmed, destabilized, knocked out, or even killed the enemy. David had prepared himself through much practice. He was especially confident because of God's anointing upon his life.

David chose these three items that seem plain and ordinary. People would not ordinarily use such when going to battle, especially against an eleven-foot giant. Although David had three items, he only used two of them. He dismissed a suit of armor for a staff, five smooth rocks, and a sling. These items were plain and simple. But David knew that the anointing of God would make the difference on the items he chose to use.

God's way is not like man's way. He "chose the foolish things of this world to shame the wise." He "chose the weak things of the world to shame the strong." He "chose the lowly things of this world and the despised things—and the things that are not—to nullify the things that are, so that no one may boast before him" (1 Cor. 1:27–29 NIV). Can you imagine what was going through Saul's mind? Saul realized that David was much too young to consider fighting the giant. Not only that, but he was going out to fight with rocks and a sling. Perhaps Saul was thinking that David would be eaten alive. That's the way it is in life. We are so prone to go to the bank when we need a loan, or to call and get an advance over the phone, that we feel that the way the world operates is the appropriate way. But God will manifest Himself in a situation using plain procedures and operating in a righteous way according to His Word.

God does this so that no one can boast or brag about what they have done. If we are in tremendous debt and financial institutions bail us out, who is going to get the glory? But if God delivers us from a hopeless situation, He will get all the praise and the honor as well as the glory! David used what he had and allowed God to show the world that God was faithful.

CHAPTER 8

Goliath's Reaction (1 Samuel 17:41–44)

When the Philistine giant got close to David and saw that he was just a boy, he was disappointed. Goliath expected his challenger at least to be a man. He felt that he had no competition at all. When we are dealing with debt, it is the small purchases we overlook that would actually help us get out of our situation. Many times, we want better jobs paying more money, only to create more debt. An experienced, strong, and intelligent soldier is not needed in this situation. Getting out of debt is not dependent on our strength, experience, or intelligence; we need God!

The giant began cursing David's God. He said, "Am I a dog, that thou comest to me with staves [sticks]?" (1 Sam. 17:43). This can happen if you take the David Debt Management approach. You will be ridiculed for wanting to be conservative and use less of the world's resources. Unpaid debt will come back to haunt you. The giant will call you on the phone to remind you of what you owe. Not being able to pay your creditors will cause you to go into hiding. It will cause you to do things that you would not ordinarily do.

David's Response (1 Samuel 17:45–47)

David heard what the giant said and listened patiently. Immediately after Goliath finished talking, David began to share with him what he was going to do to him. David responded to the giant with a prophecy: "You came here with a sword, and with a spear, and with a shield: but I come to thee in the name of the Lord of hosts, the God of the armies of Israel, whom thou hast defied" (1 Samuel 17:45). In a similar way, you must know what you are going to do about the indebtedness that you have incurred. You must have a plan for how you will liquidate the debt. In order for you to deal with debt, you will need to do the following:

1. Operate in the name of the Lord (walk in faith according to His Word)
2. Acknowledge who the Lord is
3. Realize that debt brings shame

Operate in the Name of the Lord
David operated in the name of the Lord. He discovered from the situation with the lion and the bear that there is power in the name of the Lord. God's name alone brings defeat to the enemy. All the Israelites' enemies in Jericho heard about the name of God and how He had brought Israel out of Egypt, led them across the Red Sea, drowned the enemy, and destroyed the kings of the Amorites. As a result, their "hearts melted; neither did there remain any more courage in anyone" (Josh. 2:10–11). Even in the New Testament, God's name is held in high regard, "that at the name of Jesus every knee should bow, of those in heaven, and of those on earth, and of those under the earth, and that every tongue should confess that Jesus Christ is Lord, to the glory of God the Father" (Phil. 2:10–11).

CHAPTER 8

Acknowledge Who the Lord Is
To acknowledge means to admit, confess, allow, and own up to. David acknowledged that he came in the name of the Lord. He admitted that God alone was going to do what needed to be done in this particular situation. David confessed aloud and made it known that God was in charge. Solomon left on record that we should "trust in the Lord with all your heart and lean not on your own understanding; in all your ways acknowledge him, and He shall direct your paths (Pr. 3:5–6). We should not go ahead and make financial decisions without consulting God. God should be informed through prayer and consultation or by talking with our spiritual leaders first. Don't create a giant and then expect God to come kill it.

Realize that Debt Brings Shame
To realize means to understand fully concerning a matter. It means to comprehend and appreciate. David had come to the realization that he could do all things through God. He had full assurance that God would come through for him. First of all, he knew why he was taking on the giant's challenge. It was to declare God as the God of Israel. Second, he knew that God would not allow him to defend God's name and not defend David in return. Third, he knew that God had not brought him to this point in life to leave him. Something had to be done about this giant, and David knew God could do it through him as God's servant. Fourth, he realized that this was an uncircumcised Philistine who was challenging the people of God. He shouldn't have been allowed to do so.

As the people of God, we must realize that we have the ability to do anything after God has approved it. God will never lead us where He cannot keep us. He will never prompt us to do something without backing us up. If God gives us the directions to go for it, we had best believe we can do it. We "can do all things through Christ which strengtheneth" us (Phil. 4:13).

CHAPTER 9

David Prophesied (1 Samuel 17:46–47)

David made it clear to the giant that this was his last day to come out there running off at the mouth. David had made a declaration that this was the day that Goliath would be defeated. He prophesied, "This day will the Lord deliver thee into mine hand; and I will smite thee, and take thine head from thee; and I will give the carcasses of the host of the Philistines this day unto the fowls of the air, and to the wild beasts of the earth; that all the earth may know that there is a God in Israel. And all this assembly shall know that the Lord saveth not with sword and spear: for the battle is the Lord's, and he will give you into our hands."

There are three things that David said God would help him do on this particular day:

1. Deliver Goliath into David's hand (1 Samuel 17:46a)

2. Enable David to kill Goliath and cut his head off (1 Samuel 17:46b)

3. Give Goliath's body to the birds and wild beasts (1 Samuel 17:46c)

CHAPTER 9

The Lord Will Deliver You into My Hand
David is specific with this prophecy. He informs the giant that he would be delivered into David's hand. As we know, when debt is accumulated, it becomes a big giant in our lives. Until it is paid and satisfied, debt will enslave us. Once we pay the debt off, we have control again. God wants to deliver the giant into our hands. God does not want us to be trapped in the valley and afraid to come out because the giant of debt is threatening us.

I Will Kill You and Cut Your Head Off
Once God delivers the giant into our hands, it is up to us to get rid of it. We must already be determined that if God delivers, we will execute the plan. David said, "I will cut your head off" (1 Sam. 17:46). Why did he not simply say, "I am going to kill you"? Why was he so specific? David aimed for the giant's head because that is where all the trouble was coming from. It was reported that the giant had been coming out for forty days to challenge the army of Israel. David figured cutting his head off and would put an end to his big mouth.

The Scripture teaches, "Death and life are in the power of the tongue: and they that love it shall eat the fruit thereof" (Pr. 18:21). David made it his business to pronounce that the giant's head would be cut off. That would solve the cursing problem, and Goliath would not be able to curse anyone else.

I Will Give Your Body to the Birds and Wild Beasts
David was not just going to cut off the giant's head; he prophesied that he would also leave Goliath's body for the birds (buzzards) and the wild beasts (opossum). When you are coming out of debt, make sure that you have a full understanding of your financial situation. Make sure you have receipts to verify that you have made payments. Especially be sure to keep the paid-in-full receipt.

CHAPTER 10

Why Pay off Debt? (1 Samuel 17:46b–47)

David wanted everyone to know that God could beat this Philistine giant. God used David to show Israel that He was not pleased with the giant defaming His name. David was going to make sure that God's good name was restored. David was saying, "When I defeat you, everybody will know that there is a God in Israel. Not only that, but they will know that you were defeated with a sling and rock and not with a sword and spear."

David knew that God's name was at stake; his son Solomon said, "A good name is rather to be chosen than great riches, and loving favour rather than silver and gold" (Proverbs 22:1); and "A good name is better than precious ointment" (Ecclesiastes 7:1). Your name is also very important! When you are heavily in debt and unable to pay your creditors, it will affect your name.

David said that the battle was the Lord's, and that God would give the giant into David's hand. This statement suggests that David was at ease simply because he realized who was actually fighting the battle. Similarly, if you totally trust God in the area of debt, God will fight your battle.

David Faced the Giant (1 Samuel 17:48)

David was not just talking. He put into action what he confessed to the giant. When the giant Philistine approached him, David ran toward the army to meet him. In order to combat debt, you must be willing to face the creditors that you owe. You will never come out of debt by remaining in the valley where the giant comes out to challenge you each day. You must be willing to deal with the fact that you are in debt. Take the initiative to "resist the devil, and he will flee from you" (Jas. 4:7). You resist by taking the responsibility to confront the giant that has you hiding. The time has come to say, "No more hiding." Most creditors will be glad to hear from you. They will be more than glad to collaborate with you. There is a possibility that they might decrease your monthly amount or even the total payment. You will never know until you face your giant.

David Was Prepared (1 Samuel 17:49)

Once David came close enough to the giant to attack him, he immediately put his hand in his bag to bring forth one of the rocks he had gathered. He used this simple but powerful object to destroy the giant. Notice that he only had to use one of the five rocks in the bag. What lessons can we learn from the way David approached the giant? Here are a few ideas that David used that will be helpful :

- He had what he needed with him

- He was able to produce the object that killed the giant quickly

- He brought forth the object and used it properly

- He had more than enough

He Had What He Needed
When David convinced Saul that he was able to take on the giant, he immediately went to the brook and carefully selected five smooth stones. He then put them in his shepherd's bag. They remained there until he needed them.

When you are prepared to deal with debt, you must carefully select the type of employment that will aid you in producing an income that is effective toward depleting the debt. If you do not have the skills to obtain such employment, you can go to a community college to explore options for educating yourself to prepare for the type of employment that interests you. Meanwhile, use the resources that you do have wisely.

He Was Able to Produce the Object That Killed the Giant
Because David had placed the five stones in his bag, he was able to produce one of the rocks to aid him in his mission later on. He chose "five smooth stones" out of the brook, but he only used one. Regardless, he was able to produce or bring forth what he needed from the bag because he had placed it there. This suggests to the believer to save what God is blessing you to receive. You will need it at a later time to defend yourself in a difficult situation.

In 2 Kings 4:1–4, the story is told of a woman whose husband had died. She was threatened by creditors to take her two sons as payment for their debt. She immediately shared this horrifying news with the prophet Elisha. Elisha posed a question to the woman: "What hast thou in the house?" She said that she only had some oil. Elisha instructed her to go borrow some vessels and to shut the door and begin pouring oil. She obeyed as he instructed and poured oil until she ran out of vessels. The woman came again to Elisha and reported that there were no more vessels. He then instructed her to go sell what she had, pay her debts, and "live thou and thy children of the rest" (2 Ki. 4:7). She had what she needed to satisfy her creditors and some remaining for her and her sons.

He Used the Object Properly

David placed the rock in the sling, swung it repeatedly, and released it, hitting the giant in the forehead. The rock perfectly struck the giant, sinking into his forehead, and he fell forward, flat on his face. Because David had previously practiced using his sling, he was prepared for the giant. If we use what God has entrusted to us properly, and we practice wise saving and spending, when the giant comes, we can defeat him without a doubt.

He Had More Than Enough

David only used one stone to defeat the giant Goliath. He had four stones remaining in his bag. God wants to give us more than we need in the time of battle. Even though He knows that you will not need all of your resources to defeat the enemy, He prefers that you have more than enough. If we are wise as a serpent and harmless as a dove, we will be prepared for the giant (Matt. 10:16). God does "exceeding abundantly above all that we ask or think, according to the power that worketh in us" (Eph. 3:20).

Aren't you tired of not having enough? Aren't you tired of hardly making ends meet? Aren't you tired of living from paycheck to paycheck? What about paying out more than you bring in? Take the David Debt Management approach and turn your situation around!

CHAPTER 11

Prophecy fulfilled (1 Samuel 17:50–51)

David Prevailed Over Goliath the Giant
David prevailed, meaning to be successful or win out. David predominated, overcame, succeeded, and conquered the giant with a sling and one stone. God used these simple objects to defeat the gigantic Philistine. The stone brought the giant down to the ground, flat on his face. David was not satisfied, though. He had to complete the task of cutting off the giant's head and leaving his body for the birds and wild beasts. He realized that he did not have a sword, so he ran and stood upon the Philistine giant, took Goliath's sword from its sheath, and severed the giant's head from his body. When the Philistines saw that their champion was dead, they fled. God was faithful and allowed David to bear this challenge. Paul later wrote to the Corinthians, "There hath no temptation taken you but such as is common to man: but God is faithful, who will not suffer you to be tempted above that ye are able; but will with the temptation also make a way to escape, that ye may be able to bear it" (1 Cor. 10:13).

CHAPTER 11

Defeating the Giant Brought Joy
The men of Israel and of Judah arose and shouted and pursued the Philistines. Once the giant was defeated, it brought joy to the Israelites. It motivated those who were hiding with no hope to come out and fight. If David had not trusted God and challenged the giant, defeating him, the Israelites would have continued to hide. When we take the initiative to believe God as David did, we shall overcome the giant that we face as it relates to debt as well as convince others to do the same.

Israel spoiled the tents of the Philistines (1 Sam. 17:53). They took over their territory and invaded their camp. God intends for His people to lead by example. We are the head and not the tail (Deut. 28:13). Therefore, we should own banks and other such institutions to be able to help those who need it. The world should be coming to the church, to believers, for advice and consultation. The church has been mandated to set the example for the world to follow.

Conclusion of the Matter (1 Samuel 17:54–55, 57)

After defeating the giant, David brought the giant's head to Jerusalem, but he put Goliath's armor in his own tent. David had the head of the giant in his hand when he was brought before Saul (1 Sam. 17:57). Goliath's head represented the "receipt paid in full." David's experience with killing the lion, the bear, and now the giant shows the believer how to cancel debt.

The David Debt Management Plan is designed simply to help you cancel debt, but you must be disciplined to comply with the plan. Saul inquired as to whose son David was (1 Sam. 17:55). In a similar way, the world will want to know who we are once we begin exercising our faith in canceling debt. God's response will be, "I will be a Father unto you, and ye shall be my sons and daughters, saith the Lord Almighty" (2 Cor.

6:18). Jesse could be proud of his youngest son for being so brave. God used the youngest of the eight sons of Jesse to manifest God's name in a difficult situation. He also wants to use us to manifest His name so that we may become debt free for the purpose of ministry.

Follow the David Debt Management Plan on the following page and experience becoming debt free. Kill the lion, kill the bear, and kill the giant, and you can expect financial freedom.

ACKNOWLEDGMENTS

Acknowledgments are made to the faithful and dedicated people in my life. I thank God our heavenly Father and Creator, His Son Jesus who died for us all, and His Precious Holy Ghost who brings comfort to the Body of Christ. I thank God for my lovely, beautiful, sweet, kind, and sexy wife who gave support and prayers throughout this entire work as well as in other endeavors. I thank God for the late Dr. W. W. Williams, our pastor of the Ebenezer M.B.C. for thirty years before being called home to be with the Lord. Thank you and Mother Rose Williams for your spiritual guidance for our family. I thank God for my parents, the late Deacon Wade T. and Mary E. Ellerbe, for the morals and values they instilled in me to be positive minded and faithfully devoted to the cause of Christ! I thank God for my late father- and mother-in-law, Rev. June and Mother Mildred Hamilton, for receiving me as one of their very own and sharing with me by example. I thank God also for the late Deacon Robert and Mother Addie Pickett, our adopted parents in the Lord. I thank God for my children and their spouses, our grandchildren, and the TCIF Inc. church families.

www.ingramcontent.com/pod-product-compliance
Lightning Source LLC
LaVergne TN
LVHW012049070526
838201LV00082B/3874